Cover by: Kate Hensley Photos

CEDRIC NORRIS JR.

GRACEFULLY BROKEN

A STORY OF PURPOSE, PRAYER, & PROPHECY

Dedicated to Emily Roberson

Thank you for teaching me the very essence of what it means to forgive.

Special Thanks to:
Cedric Norris, Sr.
Sabrina Norris
Hattie Johnson
Nyesha Evans
Amber Norris
Camren McNair
Rev. Fredrick D. Favors
Mikaela Thomas
Rev. Michael Thomas
First Lady, Elizabeth Thomas
Kimberly Johnson
Johnny Gaye
Amy Poston Jenkins
Adrienne Gaines
Breya Bentley
Sis. Pecola Wiley
Thomson Alumnae Chapter, DST, Inc.
Stacey Milner
Tiffany Bayne
Elizabeth Christopher
Marie-Claire Quartemont
Laura Boswell
Tyler Bertschin
Braxton Roberts
AJ Summers
Spenser Ford
Emily Liebel
Garrett Poillucci
Kimberly Foster
Davis Foster
The Roberson Family
Valeri Cushman
Krista Jones Bonner
Margarita Munoz

Will Steinman
Jackson Sutko
Kameron Doster
Brie Marijanich
Hailey Bryant
Christopher Crenshaw
Triyoko Boatwright
Yasmine Cook
Matthew Sampson
RJ Gardener
Luke Bryant
Miranda Murphey
Sanford Caroline Neel
Tora Finch
Tammy Robertson
Liz Sockwell
Elizabeth Christopher
Michael Igbonagwam
Kay Baker Chalker
Tommy & Louise Burgess
Anita Cummings
Timmy Murphy
Mariah Wall
Sha & Montreal Wilson
Marion & Liz Crawford
Tracey Norris
Nerrissa Norris
Shan McNair
Chris Norris
Kate Hensley
Jai Fitzgerald
Nathan Lippert
Carlye Robertson
Laura Batten
Springfield Baptist Church Family

Contents

Some kind of way it was asked of me to read this text and introduce it to readers – to ease you all into the experience you would share while understanding the process of being *Gracefully Broken*. When Cedric asked me to write this introduction, I considered it an honor – but I had no clue why he was led to ask me. I mean, of course we are friends and I have known him for an entirety but still, why me? Nonetheless, I agreed and began to dig into *Gracefully Broken* – dissecting every chapter and flipping it to how it applies to me and where I am in my life.

I have never been able to pin point when I met Cedric, or when him and I became friends – which has always been weird to me. Typically, you remember places or moments in life when you become close to someone, right? I can however remember realizing that our friendship was centered around God and our faith. One night in Augusta, Cedric, myself and our friend Breya sat out by the pool at Breya's complex and started to dissect some of our interactions with God and some of the messages He had sent through people, scenarios, and dreams. Cedric went into the depths of his interaction with Marie-Claire and the prophecy she had about his life. We all felt that there was an underline meaning there but we closed the discussion by simply saying – the prophecy did not come to us, so we can only break it down to a certain extent. We agreed to pray for clarity and a discernment about Breya's and I spiritual encounter, along with his prophecy.

I personally speak big on discernment – when God gives you a vision or a message – remember it – attempt to figure it out – what is God's message to you – what is he preparing you for? As we asked each other these questions we realized that a lot of the answers we were seeking from God were right in front of us.

The beginning of Gracefully Broken takes me to a place of admission, admitting that I have too experienced a war on happiness and my spiritual peace. Being able to admit that helps 'formulate the grasp' and gives us something to hold onto – a basis to go by. Digging deeper into the text, it becomes clear that Cedric wants us to acknowledge the act of being accountable along with realizing that once we formulate the grasp – we must then reach out to everyone within our spiritual circle and ask them to gear up for the spiritual war on our lives. Often times, we miss the first step of being broken and ignore it for just 'having a bad day'. The more I read, the more I began to realize that I connect to this book in more ways that I would like to admit. As I continued into "Focusing on Forgiveness" I had a moment to myself

– a moment of admitting, accepting, and hearing God's word through this text. Before reading this book, I forgave others because it was the Christian thing to do, it was what God instructed us to do. While reading I realized that all this time I thought I had forgiven people, but in actuality I had never healed. I was still carrying the baggage of others on my back and I had failed in holding myself accountable. It was at this moment of reading, I started to experience what I needed – and that was a spiritual cleanse. Not that I was dirty or filled with filth, but I needed to be reminded of the promises God had made for myself,

for you,

for Cedric

- for us all.

The question still remains—why was it laid on Cedric's heart to ask me to write this introduction?

After reading and writing this introduction – the answer was made clear, it was even mentioned above, "*...we realized that a lot of the answers we were seeking from God were right in front of us.*" – That answer being, I was broken. And although I could sing every lyric to 'Gracefully Broken' and I knew what it meant to be broken, I did not understand the most important part and that was GRACE. To be broken with and by the grace of God allows your soul to encounter a spiritual realm that no one can take you to—one that only God can get you out of.

You need to be gracefully broken. You need to read every word and experience the spiritual chills and hear God whisper things that He's been saying to you all along. This is more than just a book, this is more than just a reflection of a spiritual journey, this story is a spiritual rehab. It puts you in the place to digest being broken. It *makes* you forgive, *makes* you refocus on God, and *allows* you to feel the benefits of having faith and trusting God in every step of your broken journey. This book will set you free and ultimately reinforce the armor of God to remind you how and why you have to fight for our Almighty Savior.

-Mikaela M. Thomas

A Prayer for the Believer's Heart

God, I stand before you today ignorant of the truth you have for me— falling short I stray away because of my submission to the worldly ways. But my love is fierce, my heart is pure, and my life is ready to be moved in awe of you. You are a miracle worker— a spirit moving so silently through the hearts of many but speaking so mightily. I am full of your love. My life in overflow. I know no life without you. I know no talents without you. You are who I am. I lose myself in your glory. I stand in shock of your grace. I know you are a barrier breaker, a healer, a provider, a father. And as I stand here as your son, I feel your hug of reassurance embracing me. I feel your kiss of kindness pressing against my cheeks and it brings tears to my eyes Father. It raises the hairs on my neck and it fills me with an indescribable, irreplaceable love. You never leave me and for that I'm grateful.

Today the sun rose, and birds began to chirp in response to the awakening of life. Dew- kissed grass was treaded upon as people were on their way, and the revival fire that you ignited in every creature began to fall upon the Earth. Greetings are granted, and best wishes are given all because the day is opened by you to send-off those who are your creations. This life that we know, this joy we experience, this peace that mirrors our hearts is a product of you. You are so beautiful. Your grace is so awesome—you mold every man on this planet to fulfill a destiny scripted by the content of your Word. Jesus, you are good. My eyes light up with tears of gratefulness because I've seen your supernatural powers reveal my purpose before my eyes. I no longer fear your promises and truth, God. Darkness may encourage doubt, but I encourage faith. Amen.

Before you commit to reading this work, I request an open lens—one free of assumptions or preconceived notions—only to fully grasp the concepts of why I know my life and self to be gracefully broken. God has challenged my thoughts and stretched me far beyond the threshold of what I thought I knew to reveal to me that there is more than meets the eye. I trust that this process has been one of the many stepping stones to obtaining my destiny, reassuring me that this is indeed only the beginning of a life full of groundbreaking experiences. In the wallow of this present moment, I ask that you stand with your arms to your side and palms face down to release any energy that is not of your organic nature. Be present in this moment and relax in the position until you feel depleted of all things foreign. Now, turn your palms over and bring them to your waist as your eyes close. Receive the spirit of Him, of the universe as it resides in a temple that is now free of all artificial subjects. This action, this moment, this form will be uncomfortable because surrendering to the will and way of an entity we cannot directly see is a different process of letting go. The vulnerability equipped with a position that essentially presents us in a manner of giving everything away works against the very grain of the human mind. However, I encourage you to be broken before him throughout the duration of these pages. Resonate in a place where your soul is set on fire and the multiplication of all things in and of you are standing in purpose and peace. *Gracefully Broken* was not a title simply rooted in the admiration of all things good and just. It was formed from being the product of glory and mercy, from knowing and seeing gruesome and greatness, pain and peace, failure and faith—all in one season of life. The Spirit in me stands in awe of the work that has taken place to form this majestical piece of literature.

I know it to be Heaven sent.

You may disagree, and that's okay.

My words are not here to convince you otherwise.

January 15, 2016 1:32 P.M. My aunt killed her father in cold blood. My grandfather, the father of my mother died in a demon infested room with cracked wood in front of an old coffee table on the opposite side of a pistol. One shot to the head. One shot to the chest. One shot to the belly. He fell on the kerosene heater that was cutting through the biting November wind as my grandmother screamed being the witness to sweat running profusely down the wrinkles of his skin. As he lay there dead and uncomfortable, blood painted the walls and agony decorated the room. My aunt suffered severely from mental illness and after years of pain and abuse to Self, she became the product of a life ending darkness. The enemy had clogged her mind with the turmoil and temptation of the world and because she saw no way out, she surrendered her body and soul to a horror that no one knew how to help her out of.

I was numb. There were no words I could cough up to describe the tragedy struck upon my family and as all of us began the journeys of grieving, it would soon come to pass that this was only the beginning of a tumultuous storm. As the news spread, tears began to drown cotton blended shirts, heads bowed in need of prayer, and fear streaked the knotted bellies of family and friends. We were left there to make sense of something no one could understand and the only thing anyone knew to do was to call upon God. I needed a hand in finding peace in this storm of pain. I needed answers, clarity, a story I could follow.

What was meant to be a traditional Thanksgiving quickly turned into a mass gathering of weeping— all boggled with utter disbelief. My grandmother looked weary. Her brown eyes were full of pain and her body bent over in response. Her shoulders could not lift themselves, her head could not heal itself. All she could do was exist. Her strength still evident, she managed the impression of tranquility well; and I was still able to sense God within her. Satan's ploy on her soul was ineffective. The love she had for her child and husband was one that was conveyed in the most beautiful way. She still rose in the morning, washed her skin, tied her hair, and loved upon those who had come to give their condolences. The memories began to resonate…he was praised for all his achievements — for his dedication and legacy that was paved from his imposing work ethic…and as good southern folk do, they refrained from speaking of his shortcomings.

****

But I knew Hattie to be the disposition of his deficiencies and unlike everyone else, I was unable to ignore that.

My grandfather abused my grandmother for many

years. They had been lovers since the age of sixteen and he was a hot tempered, muscled, mustang driving man that never took no for an answer.

To be a soldier in battle with the fists of a man is iconic. Eating the cake like Annie Mae and minding what a man said, loving him despite what he did, nurturing him even when he was sick.

How was she so strong?

How was her skin so resilient to the thumps of a man's clinched fist?

She was there. Her love was there, and he was lucky that she was wise enough to turn to God for her forgiveness and not to him. Eventually, he grew up — resisting the urge to smash his fist into her delicate brown skin. But as the years went on, her eyes began to resemble that of a raccoon and she was left with the marks to remind her that he too, was a product of mental illness.

Bipolar.

Depressive lows. Manic highs.

Sadness transformed to rage.

Generational patterns.

My mother grew up listening to the screams of her mother as she fell into her slumber every night. The rage distorted the peace within that cottage home and she bared the burden of the trauma. The wounds were forming in such a way that both women were yearning for the harmony and solitude of a sound mind.

****

So here in the next generation we saw the product of inherited mental traits. Where Kimberly Johnson experienced distress from the deterioration of her father's sanity. What killed him was not simply her or the weapon she was holding and what will kill her will not simply be the guilt or shame. It was be...will be…Silence.

Silence masks the freedom of the soul. It distances the mind from the heart and leaves you empty. Why do we choose to hide the things that cause the greatest concern? It is what we are taught. We are taught to be silent. We are taught to beat down our truths and fears. We are taught to make light of dysfunction. It is a deathly cycle of repetition that only musters up the premise for generational curses. I was convinced that this pain, one that was so excruciating and tragic, would not define me, spill over into me, or numb me from the ways of living and loving. My attempt to break the cycle is one that is intentional, simply because I see the effect of ignoring pain. It is a vicious frame of mind that undoubtedly ignores reality and truth. In this present moment, I am only able to register this as a grievance, but I am faithful that this will all make sense one day.

January 30, 2016 7:13 P.M. It rained the day of his funeral. The air was thick and humid, suffocating the already smothering emotions. As we entered the church, tears began to fall, knees began to lose their strength, and composure was defeated. The choir sang, and the service started— it was going to be a hard day. I touched my face to wipe the tears but there were too many. The usher handed me a Kleenex, but it wasn't enough. I just gave up in that gut wrenching moment and surrendered to sadness. I rushed away from the repass, I rushed away from home, broken from my confusion and anger. I needed to get back to college where life was lighter and worry free. I needed to escape. However, I soon realized there was no coming to comfort when attempting to escape pain. It ate me, ripped me, devoured me, made me bleed profusely, stripped me of my dignity, and left me looking at a reflection that was filled with pity and disgust. The night before my grandfather passed away he called my mom and talked about how crazy my aunt's behavior was becoming, and I asked my mom did she think we needed to go check on them. She assured me that everything would be okay, but something inside me kept pressing my tongue against my lips to speak up and say something, to push it a little bit more — I didn't though.

Silence.

So, there I sat in my college apartment weeping into the depths of night. There I sat replaying the last week in my head, regretting the denial of my instinct. There I sat feeling guilty for leaving my family so quickly. I was unsure what my feelings were about this. I begged and pleaded with God asking for answers, but it seemed as if I was all alone.

My mother was depressed. Her skin had lost its glow,

her eyes were heavy with sorrow and anything remotely frustrating could strike up a heap of emotions from her. When I returned home two weeks later, my home seemed gray. The love was disrupted because my mother was emotionally injured. It was then that I realized the woman is the provider of nourishment in the home. She is the queen of her castle, ruler of her land, and designer of energy in that space. When a woman is robbed of her sanity and peace of mind, so is the home.

As I walked throughout our home, the hair stood up on my neck. I had never known my home to be eerie or uncomfortable, but it had been a dark time for us and I knew we were handling it the best way we knew how.

June 1, 2016 3:20 P.M. The May Sun rose as we were celebrating my Grandpa's 60th birthday in honor of what would have been. The day started off well, but our hearts were still heavy from his absence. Before his death, he planned for us to all come together for a grand Thanksgiving dinner; so, this was our gesture towards making his dream come true. Music was playing, hips were shaking, and laughter began to fill the air and for a moment the healing energy of unity was working for the good of my people. We were almost through an entire night where there was no violence or drama, but I guess all good things must come to an end. A fight broke out between my family and time in my realm of reality stopped. I looked around at the brows being formed on faces of rage, fists being thrown, others holding each other from making the mistake of assaulting the other—and in the peripheral of my sight I saw my grandmothers face, my mother's head bowed in

disappointment, and my little sister in shock. My

family had a history of drinking one too many cups of

malt liquor and smoking one too many joints of Mary

Jane. And when Malt and Mary mixed, it released

anger in those black men I called uncle. My

grandmother demanded that we never have another

event in honor of her or my grandfather, and that

saddened me. I was disappointed, angry, and

embarrassed because my family once again had

allowed the suffocation of silence to overrule the

power of love. No one was willing to be the bearer of

bad news, to be the addresser of the pain that was so

evident...so it continued to haunt us.

June 25, 2017 5:07 P.M. My dear friend Emily has gone on to stand beside our Lord and Savior. This is the third death of a loved one in the past year and a half. I am wondering what God is looking to teach me from all of this. I'm starting to understand that the loss of others is a sacrifice we have to make as Christians. God only gifts His creations to us. While my heart still hurts, the treasure known as Emily Roberson was one that could lift the poor man's head and cure the rich man's greed. She was the marker in my life that urged me to see beyond the surface of people's actions. I remember one night in particular—a cool Spring night where the breeze was subtle—Emily and I went to front campus to sit in the rocking chairs. As we exchanged frustrations, there was a slight moment where Em paused and looked up at the star filtered sky. In that moment, I remember feeling this comfort in the pit of my belly, almost as if

I was looking at an angel from the Lord himself. Em said, "Mhm` Ced. I'm telling you, I love that man Jesus. I can't wait to be with Him." I chuckled, assuring her she had a lifetime to go before that happened. Well, I guess God had other plans. I never told anyone this, but I thought of Emily moments before I got the call that she had passed. I even called her—something tells me she was already with Him by then. Going to her funeral and bearing witness to all the lives she touched was something that warmed my heart. I can feel her presence now. Today and every day, I thank Em for moving my life in a way where I could forgive others and myself. She taught me to listen for what others were truly saying, to see beyond their imperfections. She taught me to focus on forgiveness. It has been the <u>best</u> gift so far. Rest in peace my friend. <3

June 27, 2017 10:00 A.M. Lately I've been having these very vivid and scary dreams of serpents attacking me. Sometimes the dreams seem so real that I jolt out of my sleep in panic, as if a snake is really after me. I've asked Mom and Grandma about these dreams and they just keep saying that someone its someone around me…to watch my back. I don't doubt that what they're saying isn't true, but the serpent almost seems worried about me. As if it's trying to keep me away from something or someone. I'm praying that all of this makes sense. It really seems as if I can't catch a break. I just can't figure out what God is trying to tell me. Is he warning me? Is someone close to me in danger? I'm really not sure. Coincidentally, I listened to T.D. Jakes' sermon "Believe", and he talked about Exodus 4: 1-6 where God told Moses to take the staff and throw it on the ground. The staff turned into a snake and Moses ran.

God then commanded him to pick the snake up by the tail and it turned back into the staff. I know that in this point of the Bible, God has sent Moses to Egypt to save the Israelites from the harsh conditions of slavery. Moses seemed to have this lack of confidence about himself, like he was not worthy or capable of doing such a task. He didn't believe in himself. He didn't believe that God could do the work in him. It made me wonder…maybe I'm not really knowledgeable of ALL the ways God moves in and through me. Maybe I need to stop running from the snake…but how? I'm trusting God will come through with all of this…'cause I'm feeling a little helpless.

June 30, 2017 2:55 P.M. Today, I heard the voice of God like I have never heard it before. In the midst of my workout I was listening to a worship song, For Your Glory by Tasha Cobbs. As the song played, a voice in the very distance of my thoughts began to grow more prominent. The voice was one that was mighty yet so still, graceful yet so commanding, and it said to me more than once, "Trust me. Everything you have asked of me I am about to give you." I knew in that moment it was Him. There was no question of what that feeling was, what that voice was. I have been praying for God to keep me on his path of righteousness. For Him to make me the example, the miracle, through which He worked through for the betterment of His kingdom and His people. I knew it was nothing short of Him to directly come to the place where all of me was invested—my mind. It brings so much comfort to know how well He knows me. I don't know what He is doing or bringing or taking away, but I trust that it will all work together for good. Life has not been the best this last year, but I am still grateful to be serving Him. I will not let my faith die. I have to keep fighting. I know before anything else, especially after today, that He is there fighting alongside me.

July 7, 2017 4:32 P.M. When I woke up Wednesday morning the first thing I did was got on Facebook. (I really have to stop doing that.) The first video that popped up was some crazy guy in the wilderness doing a tutorial on how to kill a snake. The guy sneaks up behind the snake and grabs it by its tail and whips it like a belt. Apparently, the vibration goes against the vertebrae of the snake and crushes the brain. Ew. It is super crazy though how I just listened to that podcast last week about Moses doing the same exact thing to the snake he saw in the wilderness. God is trying to tell me something. I can feel it. Plus, Tuesday night (the night before) I had another dream of the serpent. This time I was running, but eventually I stopped and ended up in the fetal position beside a tree. I believe at this point both parts of my brain know I am fed up with dreaming of this freaking snake, so something in me tells me to believe in myself. I somehow gained the courage to stand up and face it, and the more I grew confident in my ability to slay it, the more this white light shined from the core of my body. It was crazy. The serpent scaringly scurried away and then I woke up. I feel like this isn't the last I'll be seeing of it, but I did learn something from it. I realize now that I have to stop running from my destiny just because I come upon obstacles I am in fear of. The light radiated from my core because I am a product of the Holy Trinity. They are all a part of me in some way. Thinking about all of this has me feeling that this must mean something. God is preparing me. The very snake that became a rod in Moses' hand was the very rod he split the Red Sea with. God was asking me to stand up, to grab, to fight the very thing I had just got finished running from. I feel he's equipping me with a skill that will be put to great use. I'm going to continue to think on this. Who knows...maybe I'll write another book about it.

Just kidding. There's no way I can do another book in less than a year.

August 22, 2017 was a day that changed my life. On this day, I stepped into a dimension that transcended all things made by and of man. This moment in time is why you have this book in your hands. It is the Definer, the Creator, the Maker, of every word.

So, I ask of you, for the final time to leap into this spring of Faith alongside me. Transcend the limitations of what *"they"* say, so that you may bear witness to how He moves.

August 22, 2017 9:00 P.M. I am in the midst of
worship, a young woman by the name of Marie-
Claire gently touches my shoulder. She explains the
urgency of the message God has placed upon her to
give to me. As she begins to unfold the truths of this
deity, she reassures me that the boldness and wisdom
God has touched my life with is a commodity I
should take note of. The hairs are standing on the
back of my neck, my palms are sweaty, and I register
in that moment the words she will utter to me have
the capacity to be life changing. Beginning with
questions only God would know to ask, she is able to
articulate the darkness I've been battling, offering me
a sense of comfort within myself. Through her words,
she offers a direct message from the Lord himself, a
message that would undoubtedly be useful in every
aspect of my life. Prophetically, she explains how the
enemy is upset with the life and veracity that has been

gifted to me. Satan had a plan to seep into the very depths of my mind to convince me I was no longer worthy of the love Jesus had for me. His intentions were for me to fail, to find fear in the message God had wrapped up so beautifully. He wanted to destroy me. He wanted to steal my joy. And he was working diligently through my family, my friends, and my mind to scare me away from walking in what God had planned for me. In that raw moment, Marie-Claire saw the darkness trying to overcome me, but she also saw the fight in me, the denial of that nature. She stressed the importance of prayer, growth, and reflection. With such authority, she proclaimed that I needed to suit up in the Armor of God, so that I could evolve into my true Self as a warrior of Christ. Gifting me with scriptures and literature, she looked at me and said, "You are in the midst of spiritual warfare and you are *striking* the darkness with everything in you, but you *need* to find who you are in Christ. *That* my friend, will be the victory in this war."

I fell short in this journey, my faith was tested, and my soul was tampered with, but I have learned that my season of warfare molded me for a season of winning. There was a time where I felt empty, as if my grace was stolen from me. Laughter left my face and humor escaped my conscious—but God restored me. I've learned that God is one who speaks through pain. He speaks through sleepless nights. He speaks through truth. And paying attention to that internal conflict within thyself is the key to unlocking some of those truths. I had to program myself to believe not only in just Him, but the very words He spoke to me. [When] I gained the confidence to stand before man in His honor and on His behalf, blessings began to flow and like a river my worries were washed away.

You will never know a God, a Holy Trinity, a Lord, or an Alpha if you do not separate yourself from the flesh. It is crucial to know that He lives in every fiber of your being. From the way you talk, to the way you walk, from the way you behave, to the way you respond, it is all in Him. God sent me the training equipment to prepare for war on His behalf. He made a believer out of me by proving that I was nothing without Him. He is the source of all light, the kindred spirit that lives within all people, the moving assertiveness in our self-reflective nature —there is no us without Him. I do not deserve grace, it was nothing I earned, but it saved me in the midst of a bloody battle with Satan. I am no match for the powers of this world until I separate myself from my Self to allow the Lord to use me as a vessel. Stepping into this freedom, He has granted me power and wisdom beyond the measures of this Earth.

So, here's my divine worship in the form of

literature— presenting my life and love to You.

Chapter 1:
Formulating the Grasp

I will always say no to the things that do not honor me. I will always say no to the things that don't bring me joy or peace. I do not try to squeeze into places that do not fit me because I have the liberty to say no. And the great part about it is...I don't have to explain my no to you.

What have you said no to? What have you denied and disbanded in order to make time for yourself? What values have you rebelled and rid of in order for the personal reflection to begin in you?

God needs you. Today, tomorrow, next week, next year; He needs you to fight for his Kingdom; to make the sacrifice and surrender to the purpose you must fulfill on this Earth. Clean house—rid your life of distractions and people that dishonor who you are so that the pathway is clear for the steps to come. There are people who will trip you up, liars who will attempt to disable the value of your name, cheaters who will steal the joy you have only to ease the pain of their misery. You cannot fall subjective to the tomfoolery. You're better than that. Stop, drop, and roll. The fire of the enemy is here to destroy the divine destiny that has been built in recognition of you.

God's love is fierce and unchanging. The enemy toys with the purity of the soul because he knows how powerful the stillness of our Lord and Savior is. Do not fret when negativity comes upon your life. Do not fall even further into the destruction. When turmoil seems to be surrounding you, lift your head up and rest upon the peaks of God's hills, for that will give you the strength you need. Bathe in the sun and dance in the rain, for God's natural beauty comes through the days of weather. God is here. God is everything. God is the Alpha man needing no introduction to the room. Trust in Him. Let yourself know there is more—more to give that requires you to lose nothing but the negativity. Do not surrender to fools and their deceptive ways— know that you are better. Forget the eyes that are watching, the mouths that are judging, and the minds that are forming opinions with no truth. What have you got to lose? At this point in your life, what else is there to do but make the leap of faith? You can do it, you have the power, the knowledge, the wisdom, and the Word. It is there—written and recorded for you to take advantage of. Mark 11:3 "The Lord is in need of it" — there's an anointing, crafted and manicured just for the very essence of your soul. He's declared it in your favor, set up the failures and successes, darkness and light, smiles and tears, all for you to be trained under divine purpose. It will not be easy. The river of doubt runs dry because it is man-made, but the sea of Jesus is ever giving and loving in its nature, providing a resource that feeds the soul.

We are all gifted with a scared place in our spirits. A place that is secluded and purposely marked off from the rest of humanity—untouched by man or public opinion. A place that is treaded upon only by the footsteps of Jesus.

Keep this place alive in you.

It's easy to forget how the heart beats and how the lungs expand to allocate a breath into the atmosphere.

It's easy to forget how your feet grasp the foundation of the Earth, and how your body miraculously works together in this gravitational manner to ensure that the existence of who you are is balanced and aware of the outside world.

It's easy to forget how your hands are perfectly crafted for working, and how the brain electrifies to generate ~~thousands~~ millions of inter-psychological connections.

But remember that our temple is home to some of the greatest miracles. We have to learn to appreciate the instrument that we live through, to thank God for the ability and privilege to just walk on this Earth.
We are products of our own hearts and with that comes the power to choose a life that fights for

Christ. Don't become complacent. Give life everything, even when no one in it has anything left for you.

We have to refrain from believing we are not enough. We sit and dwell and get lost in the moment of it all, forgetting that the scars of our souls have been heavy in healing for centuries. As believers, we stand in a war on a broken bridge of untruths spewed and stirred by the enemy—and his main goal stands to destroy. It is so important to be present in the firmness of reflection and repentance. To go before yourself and the divine order to ask for forgiveness. Build up the tower of truth and righteousness, not for anyone else but for yourself.

Be clear about what your foundation consists of. Unpack the depths of your pain and dig into the core of it to become clear on who and what you were so that you may find who and what you are. Selfish love is the best love, because it presents an opportunity to be strategic in the planning of what is ahead. Trying to explain to an individual why you love yourself more than them is inexplicable, especially when the level of growth you're obtaining is out of their field of curriculum. If you are able to stand in the truth and understanding of why your story is your story, it won't ever go for being validated by any outside sources other than God. When God molds you and places you in situations that are for your good, trying to explain it to a hater is impossible. Why? It's not for them. What God has for you is for you. Begin to take responsibility for situations that you allow to disrupt and destroy the solidarity of your foundation and know that the only way anything was ever put by the wayside was because you failed to hold up your side of the spiritual bargain.

Accountability. An important framework that must be incorporated in the internal process of maturity. There was a time in my mind where I thought blessings were going to flow just because God was good. If I prayed, gave some money to the church, and were nice to people—my life would be easy. It never occurred to me that work, true hard work, was a necessity for gaining any type of advance in life. When there is a divine order placed upon you, you do not get the luxury of being average. There is pain you must experience, tears you must cry, feelings you must feel, people you must cut out of life—all to which will work together for the betterment of you. You have been crafted, molded, majestically placed and winded up by God to be sent on your way. There is an anointing over your life because what you have to offer is unlike any other human. It is special, and God does not treat special things in a bad manner. Accountability is meant to be full of love and being fearful of that hinders our growth. Be willing to experience the discomfort that comes with knowing that your temptations will be challenged. We tend to shy away from accountability because we are ashamed of our struggles. It is difficult to address shame that is silenced, so begin to embrace the truth of your circumstances. Born on and in this Earth, we are beatified to the sin of this world, even when our hearts are pure. Stop waiting for the process to become enjoyable, it never will. The humility is brutal, gut wrenching, yet life changing, so honor yourself in a way that reinforces integrity and perspective from a frame-set that is far bigger than that of society.

Accountability in the spiritual sense means that you are being held responsible through the grace of free will to determine the course of your life. There are certain tasks you must fulfill, lessons you must learn, things you must see before God is able to give you what you need. The simplicity of it lies within surrendering. It does not lie in what you do in and of the world—it is what you do for yourself. If God has never seen you subtract yourself from a man-made equation, how can He trust you to be a warrior on His battlefield? There is a sacrifice behind obtaining any blessing in life and in order to gain it, you must be responsible for your actions. Understand, there is a Kingdom in name of you. A place where all things are syncopated to be aligned with your destiny. You have to be clear about what you want and what you need, and in that be able to decipher between what the flesh is saying and what your spiritual conscious is saying. When your flesh speaks to you, it offers a sticky, unstable foundation –one that will only last for a temporary amount of time. But, when your spiritual Self is speaking, it gives you clarity and stability in every challenge you are taking on. The enemy will work to cloud your perception so that he can block you from seeing the blessing God has in place for you. You will feel things you have never felt. Hear thoughts in your head that you never knew existed. Do things you have never done. He is messy in his mischief, and if you do not prepare yourself with the armor that it takes to fight the poison he attempts to inject in you, then you will lose.

You. Will. Lose.

Jeremiah 17: [10] "I the Lord search the heart and examine the mind, to reward each person according to their conduct, according to what their deeds deserve."

Accountability. God sees and knows the heart. He is aware of the thoughts that are present, the secrets that are housed, and the deceit that is lingering. On any given day I believe He tests how great we actually think He is, by seeing where we turn in the midst of chaos. He has covered us in righteousness, love, peace, and glory; gifted our land with food and shelter; given our lives a turnover we never knew was possible, and now it is our responsibility as the servant to praise Him.

Envision life like a palace, something of monetary and materialistic value. The palace could burn away, flood out, or simply just rot to hell. But, if the body living in the palace is clear about what it takes to build a new home, then there is no frustration over the lost things. Because they are just things, because they hold no value in the Kingdom of Heaven, God has no problem with ripping them away. He needs to see your heart. If your heart is in the right place you will be so secure in your intelligence of faithfulness that you will have the willpower and knowledge of building an entirely new home. God is not what we see, He is who we are. Our grace is placed upon us and kept in the comfort of our souls to show that the physical things are merely illusions. It is about what's within, that is why He speaks to us through worship, prayer, and thoughts because the internal, if handled with intent and care can never be affected by the external.

 In every context, you are the fuel that powers

the very things around you. It is all about learning how to take a moment, whether good or bad, and digesting it as an experience that was intended to be meaningful and purposeful by the universe.

Throughout my twenty years on this Earth, I've seen more than the average young adult. The demons of suicide, death, betrayal, and denial have all been unwelcomed guests at the footsteps of my door. And even though my life is better now, there were lessons that came with the pain. Suicide, arguably the nastiest of them all, was a constant war between questioning life and death, only to ultimately feel as if I were not worthy. Depression and anxiety were accessories to the tragedy, making me feel as if every day was my last. Sickness. Tears. Lost. Anger. Agony. However, the greatest lesson I learned amidst the tender age of 18 was to take control of life.

Formulate the grasp.

Establish a firm stance and pull it back in alignment with your favor.

There were days where the darkness reigned in my presence, filling my soul with so much trauma. I did not have control of my thoughts or emotions and every day, whether I realized it or not, I was partaking in an act of demolition that ultimately would kill me. "Demon daze"—a term I use for describing how Satan uses his trickery to cloud the perception of all believers. It was something that I could not feel or comprehend initially, almost like a trance of some sort where my senses were overridden. Inexplicably and undoubtedly one of the hardest forms of frustration to fight, I began to understand that it was part of the warfare and it would not cease to exist. In this moment, I found it crucial to call upon my prayer warriors. Mother. Cousin. White. Asian. Gay. Straight. Liar. Lover. Leaving no one out, I made the choice of trusting them with burdens and sorrows I knew they were capable of handling. Life never told me where to go or how to get there, but it did teach me to make the best of my circumstances. To be held accountable requires partnership, understanding, and active listening. Begin to reconstruct your understanding of things and grow comfortable with knowing that every seed planted in you may not be of you. Challenge thoughts and theories, trends and patterns, so that you may form an understanding of your own morals and values. As we embark on the many different seasons of life, we have to remember that the people around us help us shape us. They were not placed here by fault, it was purposeful. Make no mistake, you, as are they, serve as the building blocks to spiritual awakenings, moral growth, and overall life experiences.

It takes a village.

Welcome critique. Trust your community of spiritual soldiers. Acknowledge the need for change. And choose to be present in each and every moment, whether good or bad.

God is everlasting, so just as you are in the fight, He is there beside you. Learn to transform the terror. Work to proclaim the peace. And begin to speak life over yourself, utilizing the most powerful weapon of them all—the tongue.

Chapter 2:

Focusing on Forgiveness

When I was a kid, it was hard for me to forgive others. Since I was bullied and heavily criticized on a day to day basis, I felt that I owed humanity nothing. Lashing out, it was common for me to walk around angry and defensive. It sickened me to see those who caused so much pain in my life be rewarded for being "good" students. I felt hopeless and misunderstood.

Being a product of bullying leaves you with feeling looked over, that is, until you are seriously hurt or dead. It steals your innocence, strips you of any confidence, and poses you with much to nothing. Bullying can happen at any age, but when it is present in your childhood it, by force, disrupts the construction of the kingdom that lies within you. There is a king and queen that bellows an essence throughout every fiber of our beings. And as any king and queen would suffice to say, it is crucial that you are able to explore your kingdom in the fashion that best suits you. However, if you as the royal heir cannot depend on the townspeople to gather resources for you, then it leaves you at a disadvantage. The trust is absent. The fear is present. And the anger is lingering, waiting to be released.

It takes a village.

It does not take a village to lighten the load. It does

not take a village to make it easier. It takes a village because nothing right works alone. Any great kingdom in history was defeated or destroyed because the village, the townspeople, the kingdom was not syncopated and focused on working together. Every man for himself? –No, every man before himself, because when man puts himself before himself he formulates an empathetic ego that registers the idea that "I cannot do this alone". The idea is to step outside of myself to tell my Self to ask for my brother's hand in this work.

We have to work on focusing our energy to things that are bigger than us. Life was not made by one man; it was something we saw come to fruition by man, woman, and God. When breath was breathed into the human species, they were given tasks to take upon in this world, and you saw man fail…time and time again. Man fails and will always continue to fail because that is the only gateway to learning life lessons. Man is selfish. Man is spiteful. However, when dedicated and diligent man is powerful. Focusing on what is important rewires the manuscripts of our conscious to say "I kusamehe"—I forgive. I forgive my mother. I forgive my friend. I forgive my father. I forgive my aunt. Because what has pained me has not been painted for me, therefore it can have no power over me. I forgive.

Forgiveness. The act of letting go, in exchange for being content and justified in your individual happiness. There is a Heaven and Hell for people to reside, and we do not have the privilege of marking the end-destination for souls in this world. We have to learn that forgiveness is not a sign of weakness, but rather a strike of strength. Maturity does not reach a threshold, so be mindful that the act of surrendering to anything that causes pain and discomfort is needed for growth to occur. Be just in knowing the frustration that comes with resentment and anger can no longer be posed if you are willing to dismiss it.

Challenge yourself to be better than your anger and stubbornness. When Barabbas walked away as a free man before the crucifixion of Jesus, he was forgiven for his sins. Jesus already proclaims that we are forgiven, it was one of the very reasons He died for us. When you are able to speak life over yourself and unravel against the grain of shame to come be forth him for forgiveness, it shows Him that you are an honest token of his divine accountability. We can be so arrogant in our ways of letting go, and in some cases will begin to use the Bible as a reference that permits us to have a sense of elitism. Jesus shows us countless times in the book of Luke through the story of the Prodigal Son that He will

forgive us simply because we are in and of Him.
Humans do not have the right or permission to be just
in their grudgery. Because we all fall short, we have
to be cautious in how we perceive others when they
do not live up to the standards we have for them.

When my aunt murdered my grandfather
before the eyes of my grandmother, it ignited rage in
the hearts of all my family members. It was a tragedy,
something we did not know how to register. But my
grandmother uttered words that I believe no one knew
the value of. "Forgive her, for she knows not what she
does." Your soul can still ache, tears can still fall
from your eyes, anger can still fill your thoughts, but
none of that pain can hold any teachings or
transformations if the end product is not forgiveness.
There is no suggestion that this is an elementary
principle to grasp; it is hard. When pain struck my
family, we were consumed with much discontent, but

in my spiritual journey I realized that I was no better than my aunt. Nothing human can be foreign to me because I share the same characteristics as she. There are no parts of me that is exempt from the darkness of this world. I learned that when she made that mistake, no matter the caliber, she made a choice to use her traits destructively. While it is unfortunate, it was a monumental epiphany to truly understand why Jesus was brought to this Earth to die for our sins. His sole purpose was to bring goodness and understanding that trespassed the simplicity of man's mind. My grandmother's statement in that moment was mighty because it revealed that nothing we do can separate us from the love of Jesus. His loyalty reigns beyond our ignorance, and we have the avenue to pursue the same if we surrender ourselves to His grace and mercy. Forgiveness is more than just letting go, it is the very instruction to guiding your neighbor in how to too forgive their neighbor. Leading by example, we have to question what we are programmed to think and ask ourselves how is that in alignment with who Jesus is?

It looks and feels different for everyone, because we are all different in our spiritual manufacturing, but it is crucial for growth to take place.

*****

Forgiveness is surrendering to the idea of hope. It is the process of molding and freeing yourself from the feeling that anything that happened in the past can still hurt you. There is a natural course that is essential to healing, and it grants you the permission to be happy and just in what you know your reality to be. Your spirit was not built to withstand the extremities of negativity, hurt, and anger. The process is tender, it is painful, but it is life changing. Today, take a moment and stand in the footmarks of peace and liberate yourself from the pain, grievances, and animosity of anyone who has hurt you. Forgiveness does not mean that the action committed against you was okay. It means you were strong enough, even in the weakest of times, to look within yourself and find a place where the grasp of spiritual, mental, and physical dysfunction was released.

Chapter 3:

Finding All Things Spiritual

Change me. Shift me. Move me. Take me. Even when I have no sense of self, replace me to make enough room for me. It is more than I in this mind. Every part of me relies on me so I must be aware of my Self.

Being receptive to all this, all that exists; work to understand that your perception of it, your understanding of it, is all controlled by your mind. It only reaches as far as its seen, heard, felt, and touched.

We serve as the co-creators to our destinies. Every moment is a permitted chance to grasp our realties back from those things outside of us. A true sense of self is more than just knowing who you are, it is knowing what you deserve. Accept the fact that you are not meant to be ordinary. No place will fit you, or fully honor you in the way you want it to. It is not supposed to—exceptional figures are not shaped for commonalities. Seek the place in you that is untouched—a place that was formed in and of you in the comfort of your mother's womb. It is there. It does not beg to be found, or appear to be attainable, but when a shift is made in the mind, the ruler of all bodily actions opens up this treasure to your conscious. Release all thoughts, all things you think you know, and let your mind run its forage for this place. Your instinct will be to oppose this nature, this feeling, but trust the process. The mind and body will eventually rest, and you will begin to hear the voice.

Only you know the voice of you, so listen to it. Explore it. Rest with it and see how the revival has kindled a fire you never knew to exist.

*****

You have to be willing to let go of everyone else, in order to save yourself.

To subtract yourself from everything man has had influence over is a service to you, by you. We search for ourselves in a way that introduces the judgement and opinions of others who have no sense of who we are. Be the vessel, the channel, for miracles to take place. It is not about searching for a grand prize, but rather obtaining a state of being that is receptive and acknowledging of the simplicity of life. Your spiritual self is your authentic Self, and it is not found in the standards or thoughts of someone else. To think about change is much less effective than being the change. Surface level superficialness is only signified as the standard because mankind fell into a euphoria of sub parity that defied the very essence of why we are here. Stop hindering growth and signing your lives over to a way that goes against the very fiber of your being. Work through the emotions, the hurt, and frustration and understand that what is is and what will be, can be, the moment you make the decision to take control.

There was a time I stood in anger because I was trapped in the chains of fear. Fearful of being judged, fearful of not being enough, fearful of falling. I did not give myself a space to process emotions that I knew to be resting in my spirit and they corrupted my mind, clouded my perception of reality, and left me in feeling like it was the world against me.

It is not Me versus The World. It is I am the world. The world is me. Everything I know to be true lies at the center of my collected experiences and it serves me in a way that only I know to be true and just. The presentation, the preparation, the purpose is not for anyone else. My fear was controlling me, even in my success, it was dictating a detour in my near future, pushing me away from the work I was put on this Earth to do. No longer do I allow myself to fall in fear of things unexplored.

My father is my weakness. He is the person I love most yet fear. The way we love is different, and because I never felt the shift in his way of loving me, the way I suspected he felt mine, it set me on fire. There was a time where I felt he did not love me. A time where I felt he did not understand who I was as my true, sensitive, emotional, and vulnerable authentic self. It frustrated me. I am *the* extension of him. I carry his name, his legacy. Why could he not figure me out? Understand me? I carried this burden with me throughout many relationships, and more often than not treated others unfairly because I was unclear about the work that needed to be done within myself. I was cowardly avoiding those hard and uncomfortable places within my Self because I was too scared to dig them up. In my immaturity, I settled for thinking of only what benefited me—never wanting to take the risk of submerging myself in the depths of my truths. Living in a state of trying to prove myself to everyone but my Self became exhausting, and I knew that if I wanted to present my Self as the example, the vessel, I needed to be more aware of what was taking place within me.

I began to realize and hear my father beyond just the words he spoke to me. I sought the origin of them, why they possessed the fierceness they did, and why his spirit rested in the way it did.

It is funny to realize that just as you *were* growing, *are* growing, so *are* your parents. Essentially, you teach and change them, more than anything ever has. There is a responsibility that comes with that kind of passion. Loving and providing for a family in such a manner rests in the hands of the man, and that can be a huge task to take on. I had to open my mind to other possibilities that reached outside my anger.

When I had to encounter the idea that my father never

met his father, it was one that opened my mind up. I imagined it must have been hard to father, when no father was there to father you. I was able to see him in a raw, defenseless form and it gave me a sense of peace and understanding. It was core-shaking to see him acknowledge that some mistakes were made with me on the way, that I had missed out on part of him because he was creating a better life for us. By grace, these mishaps majestically worked together to create a human that was unique in his ability to deliver in any way he needed to.

I began to enter into an area of possibilities, of thoughts, that suggested maybe my father just did not know what to do. And that was valid, simply because he was human. I was not the easiest, the most perfect or forgiving, and it is only fair as I am evolving into adulthood to recognize that his desire for me to obtain perfection was because his was temporarily out of reach. The intentions of his tough love and persistence were to never make me feel as if I needed to subside to these unattainable standards—he simply wanted me to focus.

He wanted me to be the better version of him. To see myself at the finish line, at the top of life. In processing this, I gave myself permission to let go, to say good bye to a past that I had outgrown and used as a crutch for too long. Wiping the slate clean, my heart resided in a place of triumph that truly accepted my truth for what it was.

My father taught me that love did not translate the same for everyone. For some it was hugs and kisses, to others correction and criticism. The challenge in this lesson was understanding that loving everyone does not look the same. That the quest for adoration is less about looking for the *right* way, and more about finding the *best* way.

I no longer allow my comfortability with dysfunction to remain longer than it needs to.

I am cleansing myself of all things cheapened and opening up a space for places unchartered.

Adjusting all parts of myself is where I found all things spiritual. For too long, I accepted a standard that I knew was inapplicable to the things I was seeking to fulfill.

We do that.

We take scraps, pieces, crumbs from the table
because our desires devitalize our patience and
persuade us to enter into a condition that does not
shape us for our purpose.

It is disrespectful.

It does not honor you.

It does not honor the higher power.

It does not honor your spirit.

If you expand to the idea of help, you will be able to
receive it, and receiving it results in being able to see
it. Wash yourself through and through, be gentle, and
know that whatever *it* may be, *it* only has as much
power over you, as you give it.

*****

Sitting in the imperfections, embracing the flaws, and
knowing that you lie at the center of truth in your life
no matter how bad the storm is, will open your eyes

to rainbows. In the beginning, it is said that the rainbow was set in the clouds as a covenant to man that no more floods would fill the Earth. This promise is one man has held near and true since the dawn of time. The rainbow has set in your clouds, follow it in its purest of form, dance with it after the rain, laugh with it throughout the days, and trust it with your happiness.

It is good.

No man has sought the end of the rainbow, and no man ever will. It is an everlasting cycle of endless possibilities we have the privilege of curating in this life.

Make the sacrifice.

Pass it over.

It will be okay.

Let go of the stubbornness. The resistance is killing you.

Allow the work to take place.

Formulate the grasp.

Focus on forgiveness.

If you asked to be changed, you will.

Chapter 4:

Feeling the Freedom

"Be kind to yourself."

As I stand in the mirror, I utter those words to myself. They offer me a sense of comfort I have often missed out on.

We ask to be the example. We ask for miracles. We ask to be loved. Yet, we don't take the time to treat ourselves in a manner that respects who we are.

Every day is the day to remind yourself that you are an inspiration.

The struggle will always find a way to present itself, sometimes in the most unfortunate of times. The key to jumping over hurdles placed before you is not fighting through, sometimes it is simply sitting, being, and standing still—reflecting on what may be unbalanced in your life. Often times we place the frustrations of life in a box, and we keep them there instead of taking time to work through them. The enemy will attempt to convince you that you are not enough—that your strength can always be overruled and tricked into being used for his intent. He plants distractions to move us away from our destiny. The negativity that exists in this world is evil and has the ability to crush every part of your being. Reflecting from a place of faith and assurance reminds you that you are capable of anything. Having the privilege of being a vessel through which a lesson flows is a blessing in itself, and in order to maintain a temple that is receptive to that nature, you must work through the very things that you hate about yourself. We walk on this Earth seeking perfection for things we have no in-depth knowledge of— asking to be changed and perceived in ways that do not honor our authentic selves.

Stop asking to be changed.

Stop thinking that the "change" will deliver you from standing in your truth.

We fail to realize that He is the power behind all knowledge, and with that comes the exposure of light and darkness, good and bad.

We are the good and bad.

To see ourselves in every way, in every possibility,

whether strong or weak, rich or poor, wise or foolish, is the example we give to the world. It is not about knowing all or being all, it is about standing in the messy imperfections of who you are to fully embrace the feeling, the freedom, of what it means to be you. The greatest lessons are learned when your fate is placed as the sacrifice. Trust yourself to know that every part of you, good, bad, and ugly is a reflection of who you are, who you can be, and who you NEVER want to be.

In order to appreciate peace, you have to know pain; simply because it will equip you with the humbleness and understanding that life could always be worse.

LIVE.

BREATHE.

CRY.

Know that you don't have to live by anyone else's

standards but your own. You have the power. You are in control. And it doesn't mean you have all the answers. It doesn't mean you know your way out. It simply means that you know you possess the ability to defeat any obstacle that may get in your way. Be open to a mindset that frees you of the chains of society. Create your own way. Curate your own morals. See the vision and walk towards it. God is standing with you at the forefront of this fire, and He is asking you to make the step of faith and walk through it—assuring you that it doesn't even have the power to touch you. The fear is boiling in you and it is paralyzing your steps forward.

We've all been there.

Fight the fear with faith. Reach inside yourself, look for the place untouched and unleash the voice of strength so that it may speak to the core of you. Your breakthrough awaits on the other side, and all of the pain, tears, and frustration will soon fulfill their purpose. Speaking your truth opens the door for change and gifts you with the peace of sitting in stillness. Defeat your giants and walk through the battle slaying the very dragons that disrespected and diminished your worth. Because you are of Him, because your spirit is aligned with a divine order that is the supplier of all things unending,

YOU. CAN. WIN.

God holds our hand. He heals our wounds. He quenches our thirst and provides us with a sense of self that is unchanging. Because we possess this spirit, we are liberated into a love that is undying. Get ready for an overflow in your life that positions you

to be the catalyst for happiness, wisdom, and wealth.
The waiting, the prayers, the fasting, the tests are all
in syncopation with the fulfillment of your destiny.

When winter storms come and darken our suns we
retrieve to a fetal position of terror—scared to see
what's next. Every road in life leads to a foreign place
we know nothing of. We have to trust God because
sometimes we can become so trapped in our thoughts
that we underestimate our own strengths.

When I received my message from the Lord, I
knew that my strength would be tested. I knew that
life would get more difficult, that my insecurities
would bleed from the pores of my body. I knew I
needed to trust those who were around me, those who
would bring me back to a place of home and peace.
There came a point where the fighter in me had lost
touch with my dreams. I questioned God, asking why

the suffering was so excruciating. The answers were not always what I wanted them to be, but He never left. He was there by my side and as I sought to track my steps, I began to see that He was everywhere I knew pain to be. I was not able to discern what he was saying to me, because I was begging for answers in chaos. He needed for me to be in a state where I could truly focus on what I needed. Sometimes we call for his presence and grace, only to leave Him in the very place we've lost sight of. I was not willing and humble enough to present myself as the one who was following. God is saying to us, that if you trust me to the lead the way I won't steer you wrong. But we've become wrapped in our own pity, serving as our own worst enemies.

We have to be intentional in our pursuing of the Lord and that simply requires us to ask for help— to be clear of the requirements we have for ourselves.

If we took more time to truly discern what God was saying to us, then we would have more peace of mind.

*****

Until today, you have chosen to move in a way that causes chaos and permits frustration—and the outcome has put you in a place of darkness. The biggest mistake I ever made was thinking that I had control over the way others responded to me. It is, in fact, in my control to dictate how I respond to others. It was important for me to realize that I could not look at myself through their eyes. I had to formulate a source of energy that honored who I was outside of the standards of my mother, father, friends, and mentors. More often than not, we choose to live in a state of being that restricts us from exposing secrets and chains of the past. We choose to pack things on to our conscious, and when the pressure reaches a peek, we explode. The explosions are exhausting, breath taking, and unbearable. And the more we make a choice to train ourselves to live in an spiritual environment that is unsafe, the more we teach others around us to accept what is as it is. When Adam and Eve made the choice to break the law of God, they acted as if He had no knowledge of their actions. As if He was not ruler and knower of all.

We do that.

We make the choice of normalizing the unbelievable--walking in numbness to refrain from having the hard conversations. It is not fair to Self to tread in a condition that drains us from being functional and clear.

There were many days where I would cry, ignorant to the reason, and in denial of the truth. My body ached, my energy was distorted, and my soul was hungry for the food of freedom. Sometimes I didn't know where to go, and that feeling, that bondage, put me in a place that accepted complacency and stagnancy.

I had to learn that it would not fix itself.

We have trained ourselves to think that things will pass because the Bible tells us joy comes in the morning. But the joy only comes when you make the choice to endure in the weeping, pain, and truth. Do not put yourself in a position where you erupt in anger because you're afraid of confronting your demons.

Walk in your truth, so that no one else can do it for you. Be aware of the moments where much is required of you. Approach your obstacles like you indulge in your pleasures. The goal of Self is to become the overarching definer of all dimensions of you so that you may prepare yourself for a life that throws unsolicited curve balls. No longer do we have to be afraid of what was or what could be. No longer do we have to be afraid of what *they* think.

We are free.

Freedom is defined on the grounds of what we choose to let go and what we choose to hold on to. Everything worth keeping is not always good, and everything good is not always worth keeping. Sometimes, it is important to make a shift even in the things we find comfort in so that we may be renewed by the spirit of the Lord. Challenges do not stem from places unknown; in many cases they are the roots of seeds either we or our ancestors have sown. We, however, in the present moment have the potential to become the bearers and breakers of generational patterns placed upon us. From spending much of my short life as a rule breaker, I know that it is in me to be the shape shifter—the adapter to all things around. It is not always enjoyable, but it is a place where I am often called out and upon to do things others find slightly taboo. I don't like the idea or feeling of my thoughts being in bondage. So, I choose to live in a way that permits me to be authentic and embracing of who I am, who I aspire to be, and who I will eventually become. The struggles I have are in some way an extension and/or reflection of the struggles presented amongst my blood line. Where the freedom factor advances is in my choice of making decisions that disrupt the patterns that has been put into place.

The power lies in the choice, not in the disruption.

Just because you disrupt the pattern, doesn't mean you refrain from making the choice.

Make the choice.

The choice to be free.

Chapter 5:

Fighting in the Armor

He was working to infiltrate my mind with fear and lies in hopes of penetrating the grace from the very fiber of my being.

He was poisoning my life with his cloak of darkness. He was trying to ridicule me.

He wanted me to believe I wasn't enough. So, he showed up in every way he knew how.

His goal was to ultimately destroy me—lead me to insanity.

I was beginning to cave, I could feel it.

The fight was too much.

At this point, it wasn't him anymore. It was me.

He had taken advantage of the foot hole, planted the seed of doubt and left me to dwell in the mess.

My flesh failed me. No strength. No fortitude. No mobility.

Hopeless. Helpless. Unworthiness.

Faith diminishing. Spirit breaking.

Fear consumed me, and I began to question God.

I began to feel lonely, unloved, and lost.

No matter how hard I tried to stop those thoughts from consuming me, no matter how many positive things I told myself, no matter what I did, the darkness was lingering.

Its musk was horrid, leeching onto every insecurity and inch of rage. Every breath felt heavy, every gut-knotting tear so painful.

Head bowed. Shoulders hunched. Eyes burning. The rush of heat rose in the pit of my soul. My agony lay dormant in the crux of my chest.

Clenched teeth. Lumped throat.

Disappointment and sorrow filled me.

I thought it was over. This was me giving up.

But then I remembered the place, the temple, the source of all supernatural holistic things. The place where my love was enough. The place where my shortcomings were only mere hiccups in the road.

Ephesians 6 :[10] Finally, be strong in the Lord and in his mighty power. [11] Put on the full armor of God, so that you can take your stand against the devil's schemes. [12] For our struggle is not against flesh and blood, but against the rulers, against the authorities, against the powers of this dark world and against the spiritual forces of evil in the heavenly realms. [13] Therefore put on the full armor of God, so that when the day of evil comes, you may be able to stand your ground, and after you have done everything, to stand. [14] Stand firm then, with the belt of truth buckled around your waist, with the breastplate of righteousness in place, [15] and with your feet fitted with the readiness that comes from the gospel of peace. [16] In addition to all this, take up the shield of faith, with which you can extinguish all the flaming arrows of the evil one. [17] Take the helmet of salvation and the sword of the Spirit, which is the word of God.

Scripture was my way maker. The healer to all things twisted and broken. I was not built to fail. I was built to learn—to fall and get back up, to lose and win, to be the force of light in a tunnel of darkness. The path of righteousness had been paved for me. It was strategically placed, put in place, and pushed in the arches of my feet to walk upon. I was the miracle, the example, the vessel to which he worked through. My flesh failed me, but my spirit, it was a gift—a powerful essence composed of matter and grace. It never lead me astray. It always brought me back to my knees, hunched over in prayer talking to Him. He was the center of all things true. God created me…created us from the dust of this Earth. We live, breathe, are a product of every creature on this planet. This life is not one curated for perfection. It is one inspired by. The goal is to be more like Him, not to be Him.

Once I focused my energy on using my experiences and sacrifices as a tool only then was I able to fully grasp my mission as a spiritual warrior in training. The treasure of impeccable unlimited possibilities was unleashed, and I was becoming comfortable in standing in my true purpose. My purpose is to be the leader, the influencer, the guider, the rule breaker to all institutional inconsistencies.

The power of that sits in being distinct, in being the beacon of life and truth in a messy world of darkness. My fight is not with my brother, it is not with my sister, it is with the darkness that sits in them. It requires me to suit up in grace, in peace, in the gospel, in the Word of God to offer clarity and perspective.

See, now I have bared privy to how my spiritual talents will be used. They are not for the structures of mediocrity and amusement. They are not for the recreational validation of the flesh. They are for the furthermost of the Kingdom. I prayed a prayer that shook and chilled my body, a prayer that requested for my divinity to be dedicated and used as the miracle and example to which He worked through. I was brave enough, crazy enough, bold enough to ask for the stripping away of all things made in and of me that resemble the world.

Today, I stand in a place of blessing and favor not because of my appeal to popular culture, not because of the clothes on my back or the shoes on my feet, but because I serve a God that says my favor lies in my ability to surrender to the cross in any moment of despair. New life does not rest in the hands of who we were, or what we used to do. It rests in the times of right now. It rests in going through the shaking, beating, and pressing of life. The oil of the olive permeates the skin of our flesh and offers us protection and strength from the ways of the world. It allows us to go about society in a blissful way, spreading favor and clarity to the troubled. The water of the Earth cleanses us and renews our palates of imperfection. We are the fire of freedom. We are the burning passions resting in His hands.

We have to learn to walk in victory—to be clear

about where we are going. He knows our name and because we can call upon Him and He can call upon us, we are instantly connected with bearing the fruit of his supernatural powers. All we have to do is surrender.

Once you are in a place where you can formulate the grasp on life and pull it in alignment with the sequence of divinity only then can you focus on forgiving others and Self.

It is a process.

The forgiveness comes by way of love and acceptance, by understanding that what once was cannot be. I have learned to practice the trait of having a heart and mind that reminds me that I am not defined by the actions of others. It keeps me leveled in on achieving my goals and living in a peace that is dictated only by God and my Self. Once that energy is focused in the right place, the question then formulates into analyzing where you are spiritually and why you may be there. Where is the dysfunction? How have you become complacent in it? What patterns have been established? Who taught you those patterns? Do they honor who you are? Do they honor God? —All of these are things that need to be addressed. God does not look the same for all of us. He is a God of many languages, cultures, and systems and we know no way of fully describing just how great He is. We have to find Him in our spirit because that is where the freedom is. Every inkling of truth and mercy rests in the core of our temple and even when our earthly bodies leave this pilgrimage our spirits have the power to carry on for eternity. Often times, we forget we serve a Leader that is ruler of all. He is bigger than any problem. He is bigger than any negativity. He is bigger than any sickness.

Put it all in His hands.

The love He possesses makes Him bigger. The shrines on His back make Him bigger. The crown resting on His head makes Him bigger. Satan is no match for the wrath of goodness that comes through His light. Remember that. Remember you fight for a God that is fierce in his deliverance.

There are no limitations.

There are no exceptions.

---

1 Thessalonians 5: [5] You are all children of the light and children of the day. We do not belong to the night or to the darkness. ⁶ So then, let us not be like others, who are asleep, but let us be awake and sober. ⁷ For those who sleep, sleep at night, and those who get drunk, get drunk at night. ⁸ But since we belong to the day, let us be sober, putting on faith and love as a breastplate, and the hope of salvation as a helmet. ⁹ For God did not appoint us to suffer wrath but to receive salvation through our Lord Jesus Christ. ¹⁰ He died for us so that, whether we are awake or asleep, we may live together with him. ¹¹ Therefore encourage one another and build each other up, just as in fact you are doing.

I've become comfortable in rebuking demons in the name of Jesus. My prayers are fierce, and they give no mercy to the darkness. I have adopted a spirit that speaks against all hatred, sickness, and sorrow. A spirit that commands that light fills the room even in the midst of Satan's tomfoolery. There is so much authority in knowing that Jesus' body was marked and carved by men who had no knowledge of what was to come. The sacrificial lamb that said I am here to gather all your sorrows and mistakes, fears and misfortunes, tears and trials—all so you can live a life of free will. The enemy will come against me, attempt to shame and destroy me even through the successes of this book, but my faith lies in knowing how the story ends. My faith lies in knowing that in the name of Jesus I am protected and secured.

There were times where I stood in fear because I knew Satan was after me, but I quickly learned that that was the gateway to gaining strength and resilience through the Word of God. I am holding nothing back in this beautiful exchange. On my knees, with my hands held high I am surrendering to a purpose that breaks me gracefully, a purpose that pushes me into a dimension of faith and discernment beyond the realms of this earthly world. My composition is now made up of His will and way. When prayers leave my mouth, they are no longer just mere requests or pleads for my Self, but rather for the betterment of the Kingdom. They are moments of recognition being lifted up for brothers and sisters around the world. The work needs to be done, and I have dedicated my life's mission to it.

You may think that your life is over—that you have no true purpose. But I want to challenge you in thinking about what that truly means. A life that has no purpose has no reason for existence, and if that is the case for you then why do you feel or love others? Why do you experience tests? Why do you smile? Why do you bathe or even bother to clothe your body? Why are you still here?

Your life is more than what the human eye can see. Every fiber of your being serves the universe in a way that even science has no true evidence of.

Formulate the grasp.

Establish the foundation.

Sow the seed.

Harvest in season.

Walk by way of the Spirit of God. Take the lessons of life and insert them into your collection of weaponry. There is so much solace in freeing the mind to know that there are endless possibilities. Trust me when I say, you have been gracefully broken. It pushed you to the end, gave you some nights where you thought life was over, forced you on your knees in a state of desperation, but that was needed. The beauty is in the fact that you are still here, living and breathing with the few who are lucky and just. Take your pain, curate your purpose, and know that God is with you.

This a testament to survival.

A testament that gives voice to imperfections.

With your tongue, speak your future into existence. Write your path of righteousness down and focus on it. Don't require perfection. Require genuineness.

You can do it.

The greatest thing about the grace of Jesus is that it is greater than all of your sins.

Set your spirit free. The grace will reach you.
I hope this healing finds you well, that you are reminded to celebrate yourself.

We are all children of Heaven. All forever free.

From light to light. Cheek to cheek. Be blessed.

-Cedric N. Jr.

Dear Spirit Soldier,

I want to know how you are doing. What are the stories of enlightenment and growth you can share with me? I would love to hear.

*Email: **norriscedric@gmail.com***

Made in the USA
Middletown, DE
20 May 2018